ALFRED'S ARTIST SERIES

TODD JOHNSON

WALKING BASS LINE MODULE SYSTEM
VOLUME 1: TRIAD MODULES

Alfred Publishing Co., Inc.
16320 Roscoe Blvd., Suite 100
P.O. Box 10003
Van Nuys, CA 91410-0003
alfred.com

Book and DVD
ISBN-10: 0-7390-5160-1
ISBN-13: 978-0-7390-5160-3

Book
ISBN-10: 0-7390-5158-X
ISBN-13: 978-0-7390-5158-0

DVD
ISBN-10: 0-7390-5159-8
ISBN-13: 978-0-7390-5159-7

Cover photo by Lucas Neuman.

CONTENTS

INTRODUCTION

Welcome to *Walking Bass Line Module System, Volume 1: Triad Modules*. We're going to take the mystery out of walking bass lines and simplify them for the electric bass, the acoustic bass, a vocalist, an organist—anyone who wants to play jazz walking bass lines.

We're going to break things down into simple concepts. One of my favorite jokes is, "How do you eat an elephant?" The answer: "The same way you eat a chicken—one bite at a time!" What we're going to do is take this giant elephant of walking bass lines, break it down into bite-sized chunks, and see if we can devour it. Let's go ahead and get started.

About the DVD

Both this book and its companion DVD are available separately and also together as a book & DVD package. Using the book and DVD together will greatly enhance your learning experience.

A lot of information in this book is included on the DVD as well; however, I often expand on concepts at greater length and detail on the DVD than is practical for the book. While the book contains all the basics, the DVD offers an enhanced level of instruction, much like having a private teacher in your home. Also, seeing and hearing my performance of each example will help you achieve the correct sound and feel of this material. I encourage you to play along wherever and whenever possible.

You may notice slight differences between what I play on the DVD and what is printed in the book. Usually, these are simply a measure or two played an octave higher or lower, or a few notes played in a different position than is indicated in the tablature. It's important to realize that both versions are "correct"; to be truly proficient, you should learn all the variations this system of walking bass lines allows for, including playing the material in different octaves and in different positions on the neck. Once you start to internalize and become comfortable with the material, I encourage you to experiment with as many variations as you can. The more options you have, the better off you will be.

In addition to the book and DVD content, I've placed some bonus material on my website at **www.toddjohnsonmusic.com/bonus_material**. This includes MP3 play-alongs, blank chord sheets for writing out your own bass lines, a "master module list" containing all the modules in both this book and in *Volume 2: Scale Modules*, and much more.

Let's go get ahead and get started.

GETTING STARTED

Defining a Module

The first thing we need to do is define a "module."

> A *module* is a 1-measure idea (or a 2-beat idea) that can be inserted into every bar of a song such as a 12-bar blues.

For example, if we take an F blues chord progression and our module is "root–root–5th–5th," then we would insert that module (or harmonic idea) into every measure of our 12-bar blues. Then, after a couple of times through the 12-bar form, we'd be in control of that idea, and we should be able to recall it and insert it into a bass line whenever we feel like it. At that point, all we have to do is to put together a series of *different modules*, and we're in business.

Strong Beat/Weak Beat Theory

The next thing we need to explore is *strong beat/weak beat theory*. Our ears put a major emphasis on beats 1 and 3; that's where we hear the harmony the strongest. Likewise, we feel the rhythm strongest on beats 2 and 4; in jazz, that's where the hi-hat plays, and in rock that's where the backbeat is. So, it's critical that we play proper chord or scale tones on beats 1 and 3.

That's not to say that we can get away with playing any random note on beats 2 and 4, but our ear does put a lot less emphasis on those beats. That's why we can "stretch" things with the chromaticism that we're going to learn later on. To start, we're going to deal primarily with half steps above and below given notes, which are also know as *leading tones*. Later, we'll make some very conscious choices about what we play on beats 2 and 4 that will complement what we play on beats 1 and 3.

> The main thing to remember now is that beats 1 and 3 are the strong beats *harmonically*, and beats 2 and 4 are the strong beats *rhythmically*.

A Good Walking Bass Line

Let's define what makes up a good walking bass line. Obviously, a great time feel is critical. A long quarter note is also very important. It's crucial that we get the maximum amount of length from the quarter note. Later on, when we start playing different rhythmic variations, we'll find that the longer we can play our quarter note, the more effective our short, rhythmic articulations will be. A long quarter note is what all bass players strive for. It's like a warm, harmonic waterbed or safety net underneath the soloist!

Three Components of a Walking Bass Line

Let's look at the harmonic elements that make up a walking bass line.
There are three major components:

- Arpeggios
- Scales
- Chromatic tones

Here is an example of an arpeggio-based walking bass line.

Here's a scale-based walking bass line.

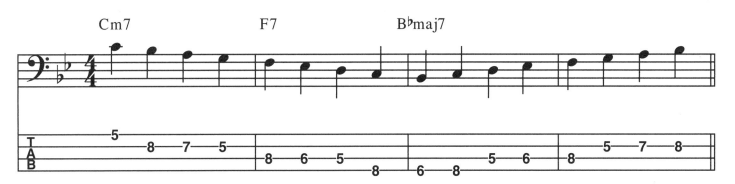

Here's a sample bass line that includes some chromaticism.

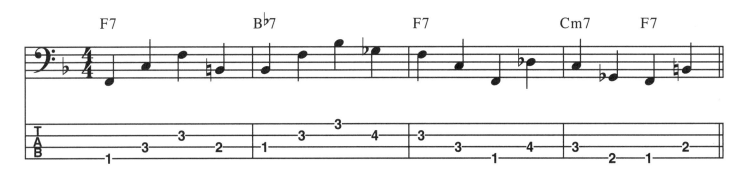

Ideally, the best walking bass lines are those that contain the most interesting mix of these three elements, so let's learn how to get in control of them.

The Resolution Rule

Keep in mind that you should always try to resolve as smoothly as possible from one chord to the next. That brings us to what I call the *Resolution Rule*.

According to the Resolution Rule, when moving from beat 4 to beat 1, you want to resolve by one of four ways:

HALF STEP

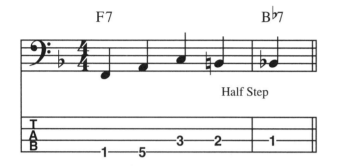

UP A FOURTH OR DOWN A FIFTH
(essentially the same thing)

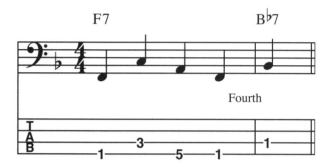

WHOLE STEP

CHANGE THE OCTAVE

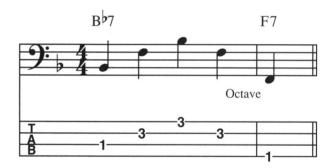

Review

1. Remember that a module is a musical idea that we'll "plug in" to every measure of a song. Practicing musical ideas as modules allows us to gain control of what we play through repetition and to file them for effective recall later on.

2. Remember the strong beat/weak beat theory. Beats 1 and 3 are strong beats harmonically, and beats 2 and 4 are strong beats rhythmically; therefore, we need to make sure to play correct chord tones and scale tones on beats 1 and 3, and, since our ear puts a lot less emphasis on beats 2 and 4, that's where we'll add chromaticism.

3. Remember the elements that make up a good walking bass line: 1) great time feel, 2) a long, legato quarter note, 3) arpeggios, 4) scales, and 5) chromaticism.

Once we mix all of these elements together, we'll be on our way to creating great walking bass lines.

HOW THE SYSTEM WORKS

Let's get started working with the triad modules. We have just a few terms to define, and then we'll be off and running, or, in this case, walking! Here's how the system works:

1 = Root of the chord	a = Half step above the **next root**
3 = Third of the chord	b = Half step below the **next root**
5 = Fifth of the chord	
8 = Octave	

Realize that 1 (the root) and 8 (the octave) are interchangeable, and it's likely there will be times when we'll exchange one for the other for the sake of smoothness.

Students sometimes wonder why we focus on half steps instead of whole steps above and below. Whole steps are more indicative of the *scale* approach, which is discussed in depth in the next book in this series, *Walking Bass Line Module System, Volume 2: Scale Modules.* For now, we'll concentrate on half steps above or below.

We have a few more rules and guidelines to learn as we go along, but we'll cover those as they come up in the musical examples. For now, we're going to start with a 12-bar F blues and apply each module over every measure in the blues progression.

The hardest measures of this blues progression are 4, 11, and 12:

In measure 4, we have two beats of Cm7 and two beats of F7:

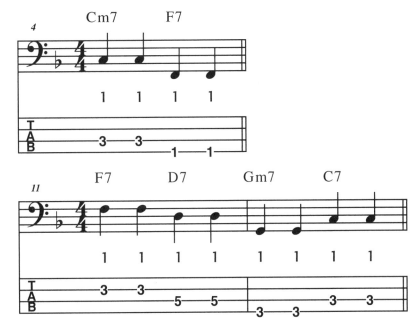

In measures 11 and 12, we have two chords per measure: F7 and D7 in measure 11, and Gm and C7 in measure 12:

Since the chords go by twice as fast in measures 4, 11, and 12, we have to think twice as fast. We'll do some special preparation for these sections throughout the book.

> **Important!** As you learn the modules, reading the examples is permitted, but only as a way to memorize the modules. To be successful, you MUST memorize and internalize these modules so that you may recall them instantaneously to create walking bass lines "on the fly." To practice, I recommend playing each of these modules at least five to ten times through without a mistake. If you do this, it will probably take one to two weeks to learn the first 10 modules.

TRIAD MODULES

Module 1 is the simplest thing that we can play: root–root–root–root. **The root is the most important note of the chord.** In a jazz situation, the guitar or piano player is going to play primarily rootless voicings, so somebody has to play the root. It's up to you to do that. If the piano or guitar player is playing an E-flat and an A, and you play an F, that's an F7 chord; however, if you play a B, that becomes a B7.

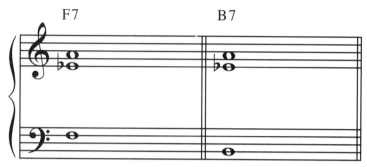

MODULE 1
1–1–1–1

As you can see from module 1, the root of the chord is a big deal. All of the power is in the root, so never apologize for playing the root.

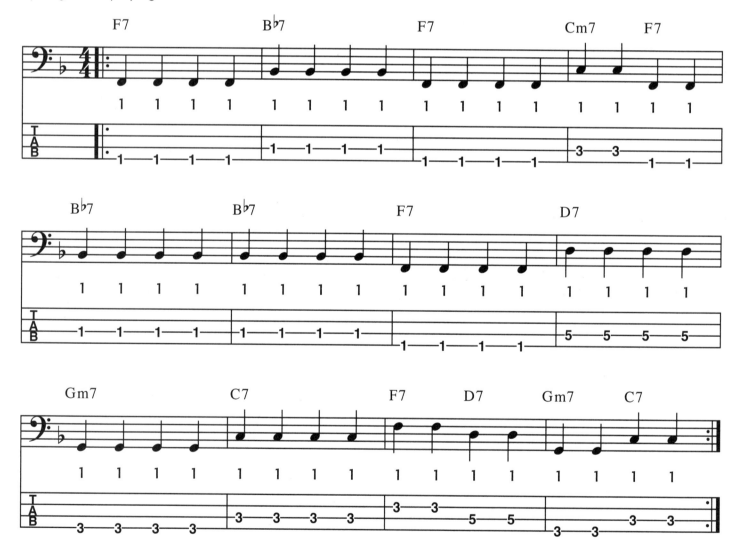

MODULE 2

1–1–1–a

Module 2 is root–root–root–a. Remember, the "a" means a half step above the *next* **root**.

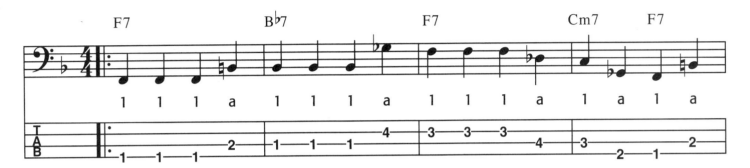

MODULE 3

1–1–1–b

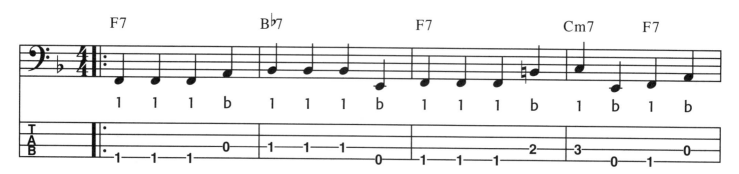

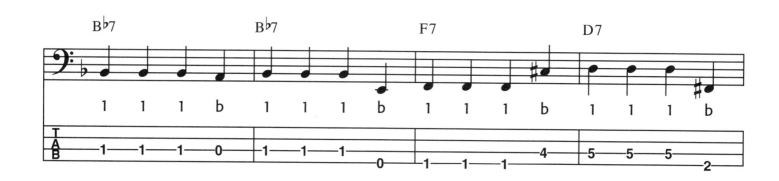

When we get to measure 4 of the progression, we have Cm7 and F7, each for two beats. Since these chords go by twice as fast (that is, only two beats each instead of four beats), we're going to play the module twice as fast.

Rather than playing four beats per chord...

...we'll play two beats per chord.

When we get to the I–VI–ii–V7 turnaround in measures 11 and 12, we'll do the same thing.

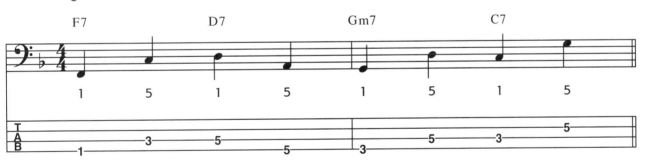

One question you need to answer for yourself is this: do you play the fifth of the chord below the root, or the fifth above? The answer is that you can play either; however, what you want to keep in mind is that you should try to resolve as smoothly as possible. That brings us back to the resolution rule.

To review, the resolution rule states that from beat 4 to beat 1, you want to resolve by one of four ways: half step, whole step, up a fourth or down a fifth, or by changing the octave.

MODULE 4

1–1–5–5

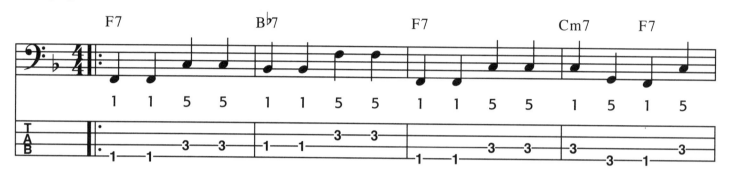

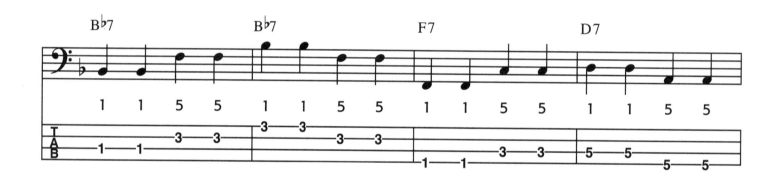

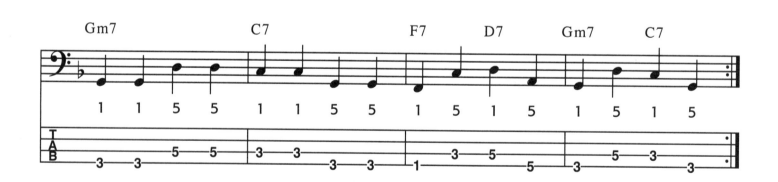

There's one thing that we need to go over regarding module 4 on the previous page, which is what happened going from measures 3 to 4.

On beats 3 and 4 of measure 3, we played the fifth of the F7 chord, which is C. Then we went to the root of the Cm7 chord, which is also C, so we wound up playing three C's in a row. To a lot of people's ears, that might sound like we got to the Cm7 chord early. The best way to alleviate this is to approach the root on beat 1 of measure 4 by playing a half step above or below it on beat 4 of measure 3. That will make it sound like we're arriving at the Cm7 chord at the correct time. We're going to use this technique with modules 4, 11, 16, and 22.

With that in mind, let's replay module 4 with this new update.

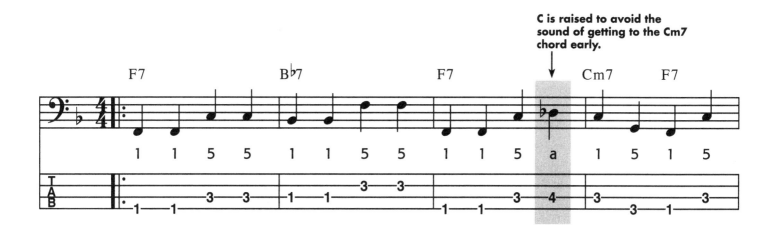

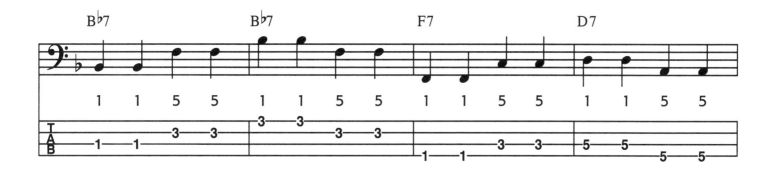

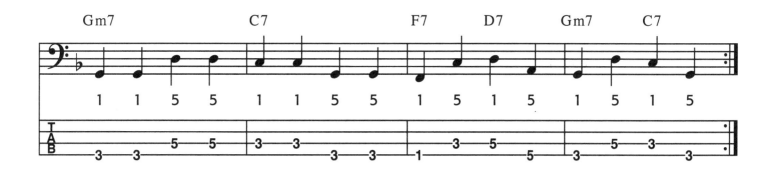

MODULE 5

1–1–5–a

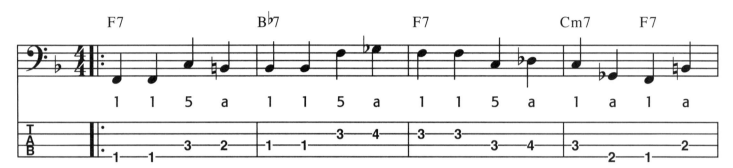

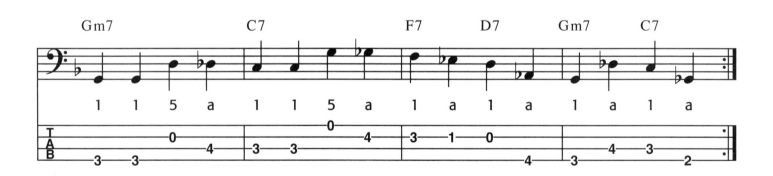

In the measures of module 5 that have two chords (measure 4 and the turnaround in measures 11 and 12), notice that I chose to play 1–a on each chord rather than 1–5. Once you're comfortable playing 1–1, 1–a, 1–b, 1–3, and 1–5, you should feel free to play any of these (and mix them up) over any of the two-beats-per-chord measures.

MODULE 6
1–1–5–b

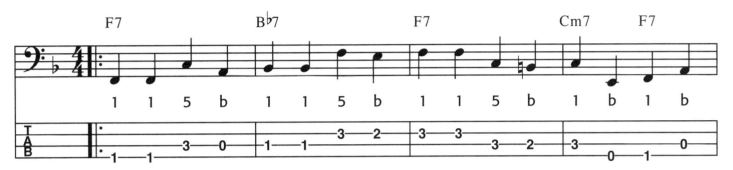

Using Different Modules

By now, you're probably thinking, "These modules work; they sound great, but they become predicable." Remember, this is a way to learn to get into control of a number of modules (or musical ideas) so we can plug them in. Then, once we get several of them together, we can put them together in various ways to achieve some great musical results. Each one of these modules seems to have its own color, not unlike a painter's pallet. With all the different "colors," we can paint a nice picture.

To show you where all this is going, here is an example of a walking bass line using a different module in every measure. For three choruses of blues in F, I've inserted the modules virtually in order, starting with module 2 (except where there are two chords in every measure). I think you'll like the results.

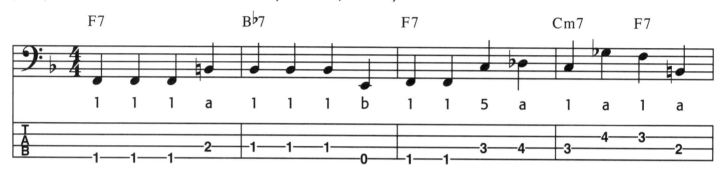

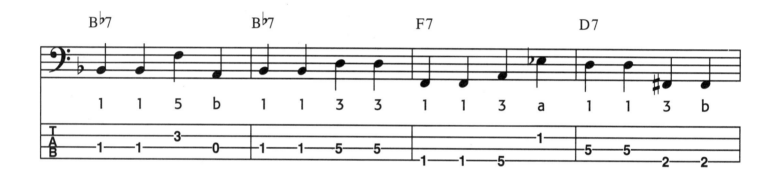

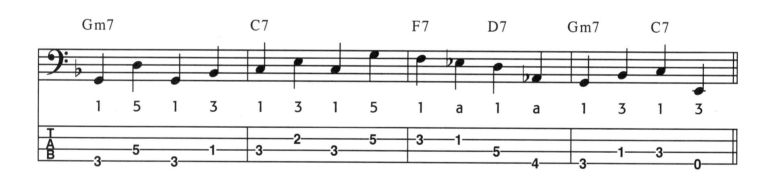

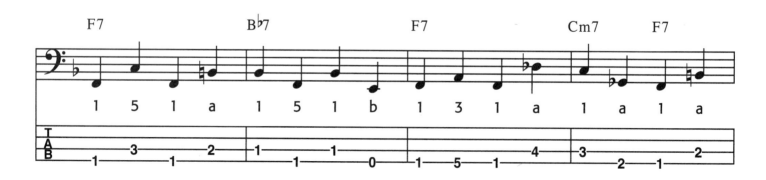

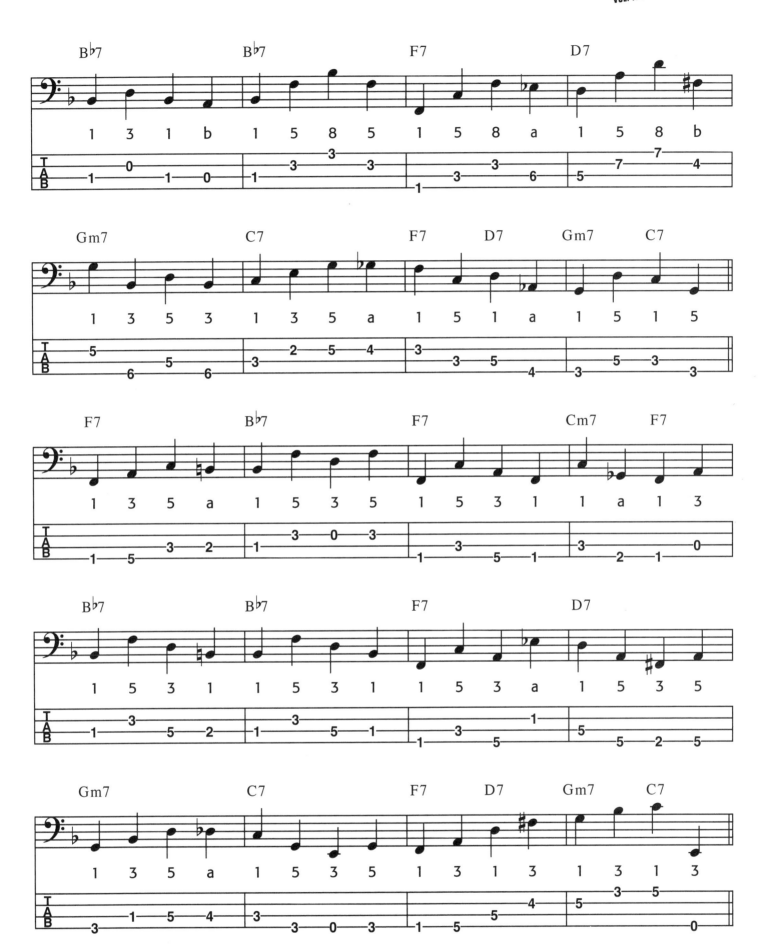

This is still relatively simple stuff, but if you learn these modules, get comfortable with them, and use a different one every measure, you will achieve some fantastic results. They start off simple, but as we move through them, the modules get a little more complex and musical, and you'll really start to hear the finished product of jazz walking bass lines.

MODULE 7
1–1–3–3

Notice that we occasionally break the Resolution Rule in this module (indicated by * in the music). Although it doesn't sound wrong, the resulting bass line doesn't sound quite as smooth. When mixing this module with others, be sure to follow the Resolution Rule to achieve nice, smooth lines.

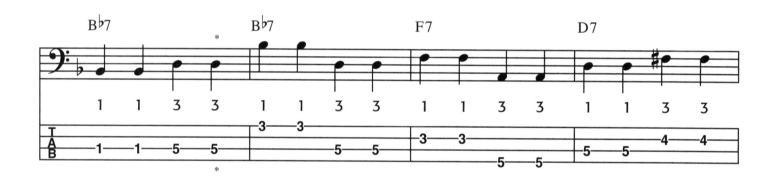

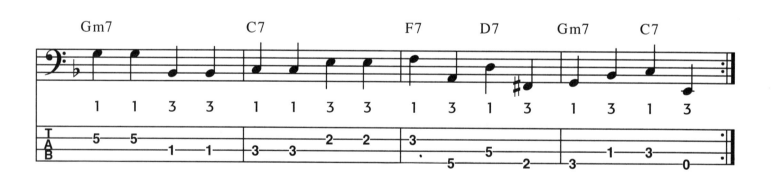

It's important to note that, if the chord is a major quality, the third will be a major third. If it's a minor chord, the third will be minor. Always remember to adjust the module to the chord.

MODULE 8
1–1–3–a

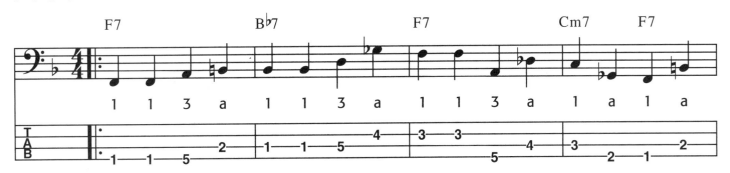

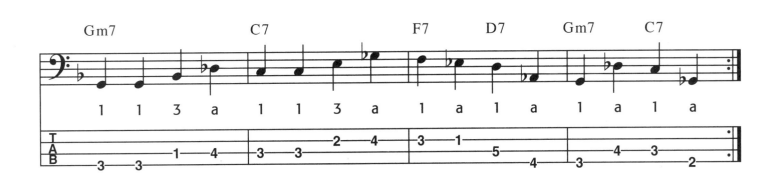

MODULE 9
1–1–3–b

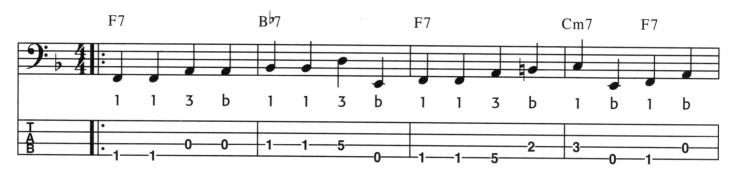

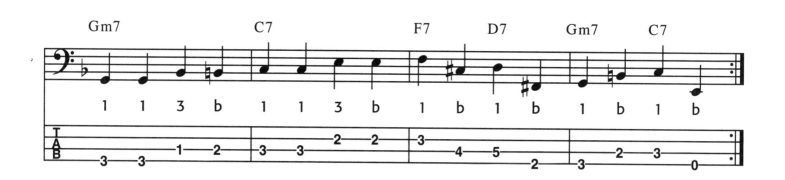

MODULE 10
1–5–1–3

Notice that we occasionally break the Resolution Rule in this module (indicated by * in the music). Although it doesn't sound wrong, the resulting bass line doesn't sound quite as smooth. When mixing this module with others, be sure to follow the Resolution Rule to achieve nice, smooth lines.

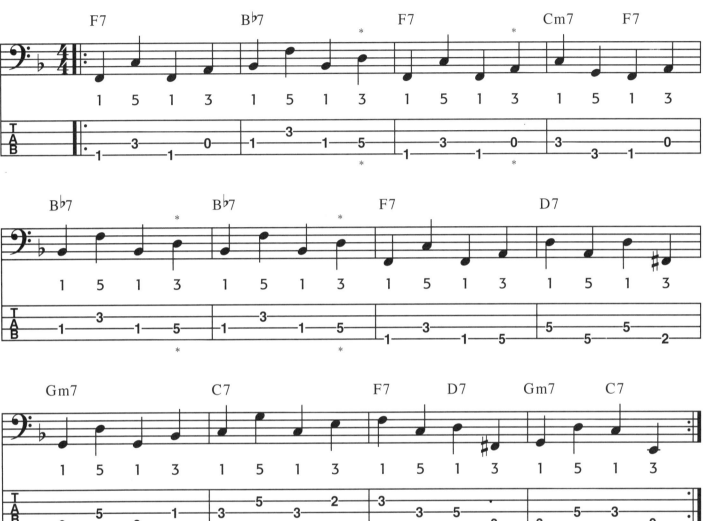

Summary: Modules 1–10

We've now gone through modules 1 through 10. Realize that the first 10 modules are the toughest ones to learn. We've had to scope out where the strong beats and weak beats are, and we've learned where all of the roots, thirds, fifths, and half steps above and below are. With all of that scoped out, we should be in good shape. All of the remaining modules should go pretty quickly, because we already know where all the information is. It's just a matter of playing it!

To practice, I recommend playing each of these modules at least five to ten times through without a mistake. These need to be "internalized"! Realize that it will probably take one to two weeks to learn the first 10 modules.

Remember! You want to be able to play these modules by memory. If these aren't memorized, you won't be able to create walking bass lines on the fly, which is the whole point of this method.

Also, reading the examples is permitted, but only as a way to help you memorize the modules. So have fun and get to work!

MODULE 11
1–3–1–5

Remember that, as we discussed earlier with module 4, when we go to the fifth of the F7 chord in measure 3, we have to approach the next chord, Cm7, from above or below.

Also, from now on, when there are two chords in the measure, feel free to mix up the modules (1–a, 1–b, 1–3, 1–5, etc.).

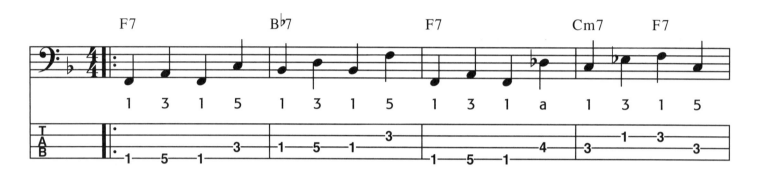

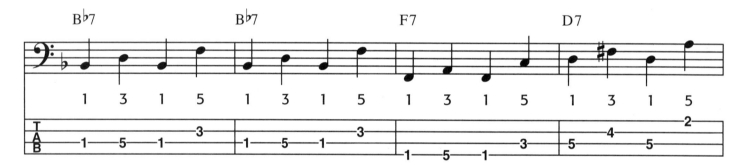

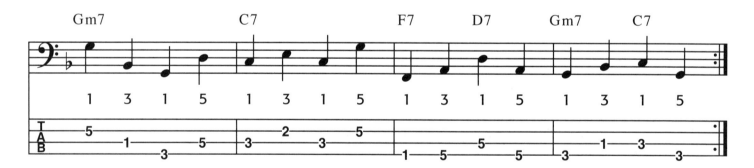

Reminder

A bass player's number 1 responsibility is to outline the root motion. Also, it's critical that we focus on playing a long, pure, undecorated quarter note. We'll add ghost notes and rhythmic articulations later on.

MODULE 12
1–5–1–a

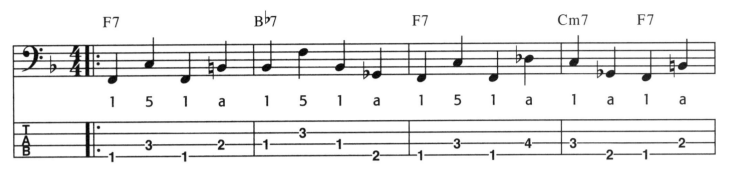

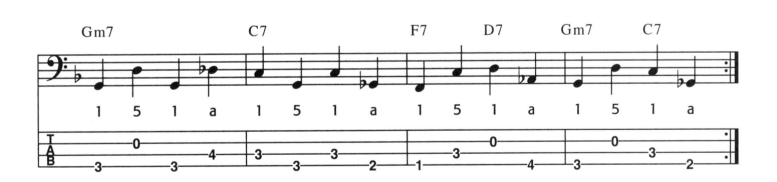

MODULE 13
1–5–1–b

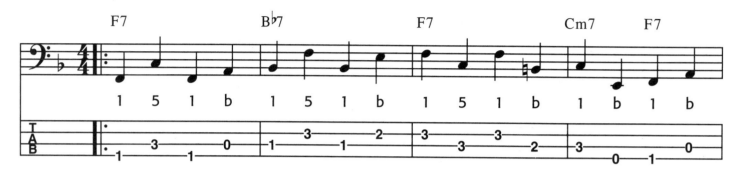

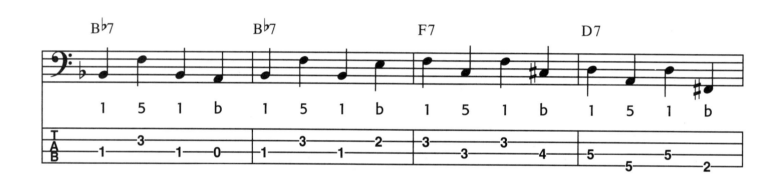

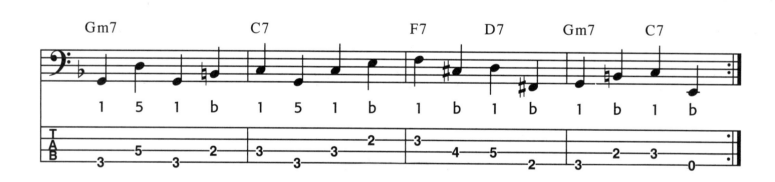

MODULE 14

1–3–1–a

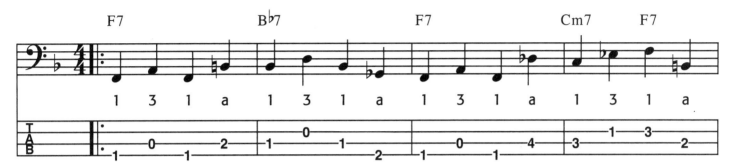

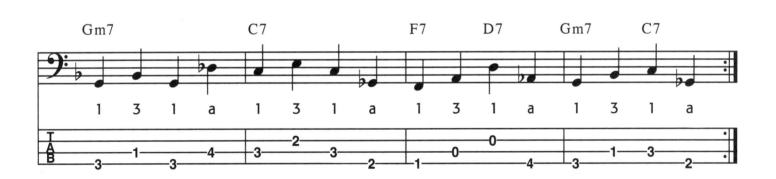

MODULE 15

1–3–1–b

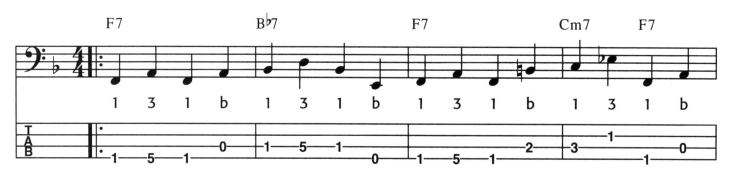

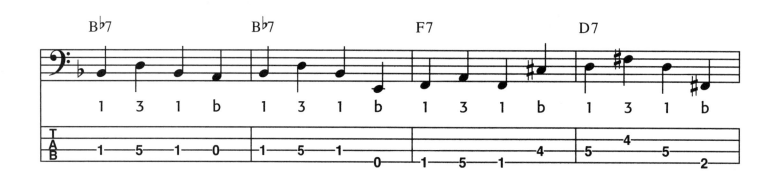

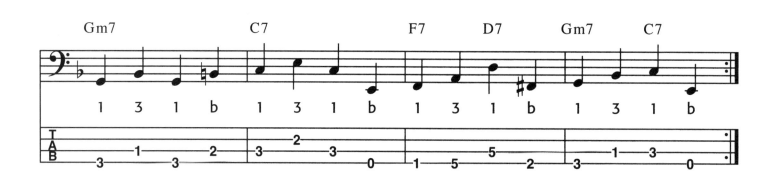

MODULE 16

1–5–8–5

Remember that, as we discussed earlier with module 4, when we go to the fifth of the F7 chord in measure 3, we have to approach the next chord, Cm7, from above or below.

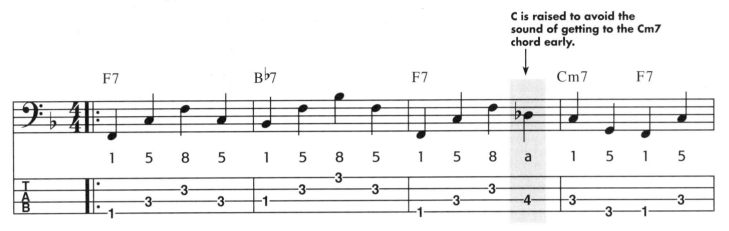

C is raised to avoid the sound of getting to the Cm7 chord early.

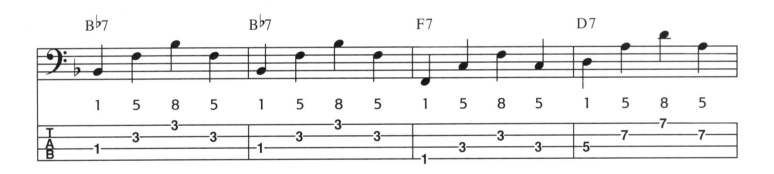

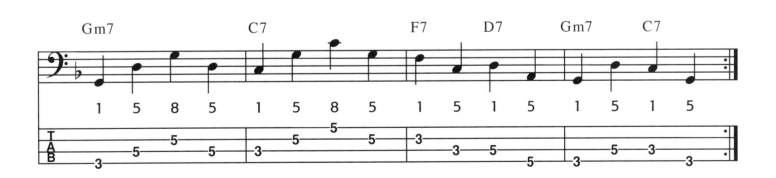

MODULE 17
1–5–8–a

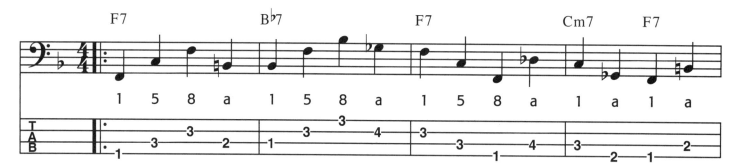

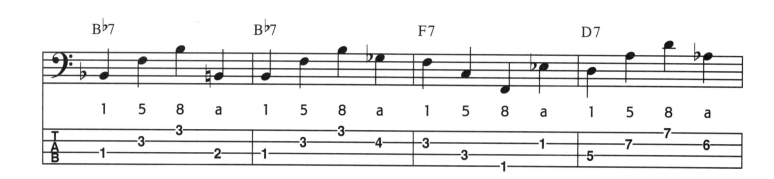

MODULE 18
1–5–8–b

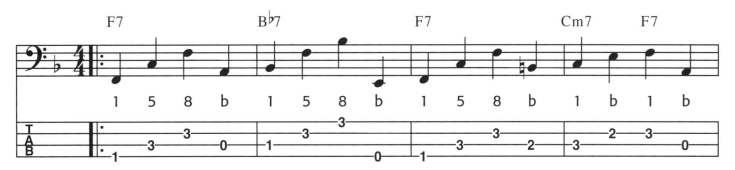

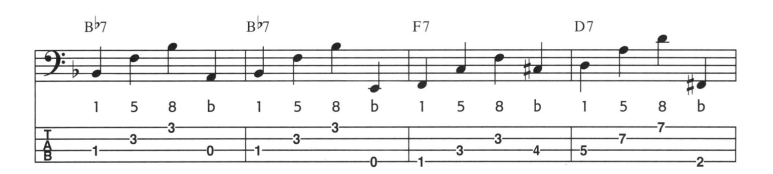

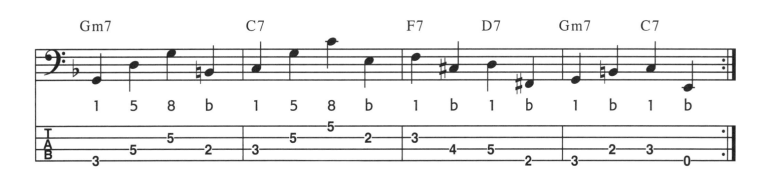

A Frequently Asked Question

Which is correct: to play an open string, or to finger the note on the string below? The answer is *both*. You need to know both options. Ideally, I recommend fingering the A, D, etc., because you can control the shape and dynamics of the note better that way; however, there are definitely pros and cons to both methods.

MODULE 19

1–3–5–3

Notice that we occasionally break the Resolution Rule in this module (indicated by * in the music). Although it doesn't sound wrong, the resulting bass line doesn't sound quite as smooth. When mixing this module with others, be sure to follow the Resolution Rule to achieve nice, smooth lines.

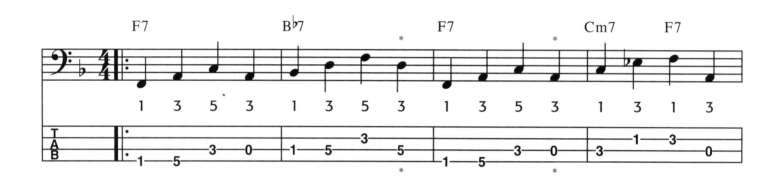

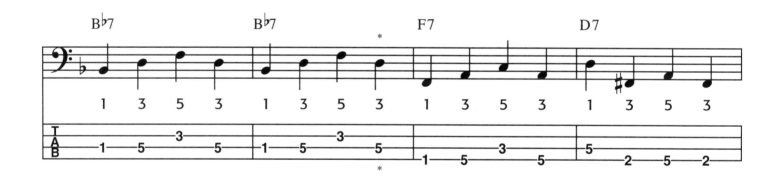

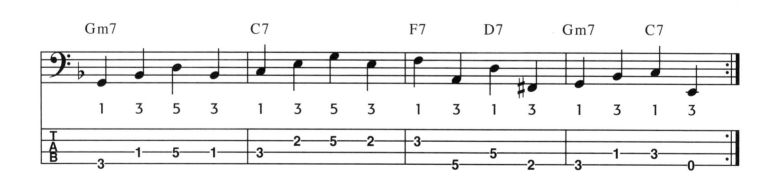

MODULE 20
1–3–5–a

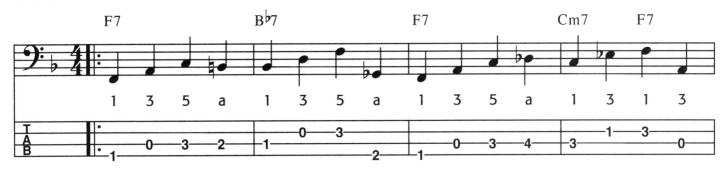

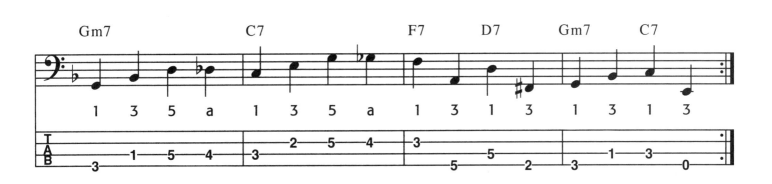

MODULE 21

1–3–5–b

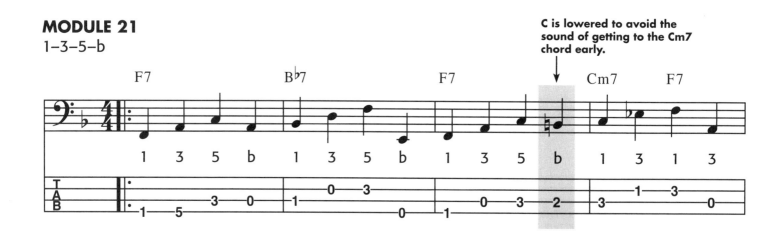

C is lowered to avoid the sound of getting to the Cm7 chord early.

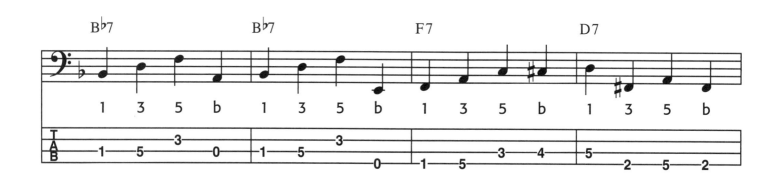

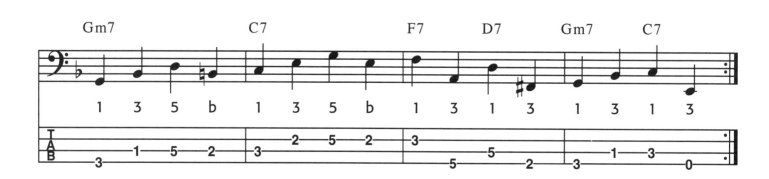

MODULE 22
1–5–3–5

Remember that, as we discussed earlier with module 4, when we go to the fifth of the F7 chord in measure 3, we have to approach the next chord, Cm7, from above or below.

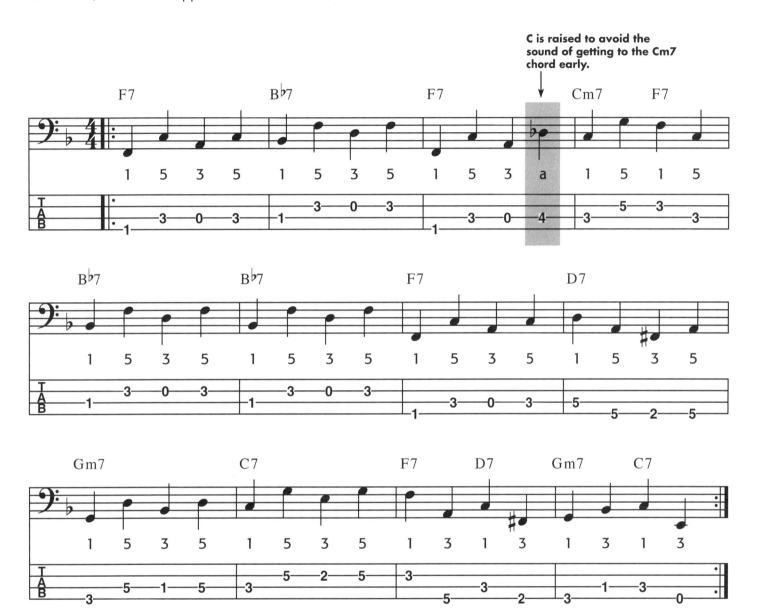

C is raised to avoid the sound of getting to the Cm7 chord early.

Quick Technique Tip

I've notice that a lot of bass players play everything back by the bridge with the right hand. That's fine, but it's such a bright sound. It's great for rock, R&B, etc., but when you're playing in a jazz style, I recommend playing closer to the front of the neck. You'll get a much warmer sound, much closer to an upright, and the people you'll be playing with will be much happier.

MODULE 23

1–5–3–1

Notice that we occasionally break the Resolution Rule in this module (indicated by * in the music). Although it doesn't sound wrong, the resulting bass line doesn't sound quite as smooth. When mixing this module with others, be sure to follow the Resolution Rule to achieve nice, smooth lines.

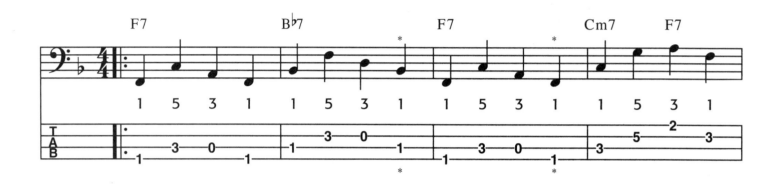

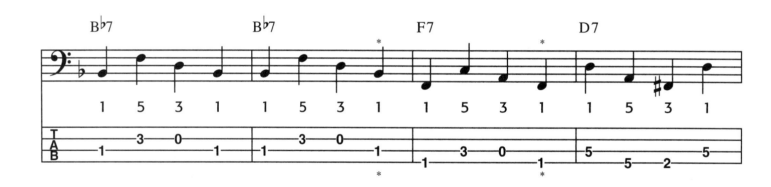

MODULE 24

1–5–3–a

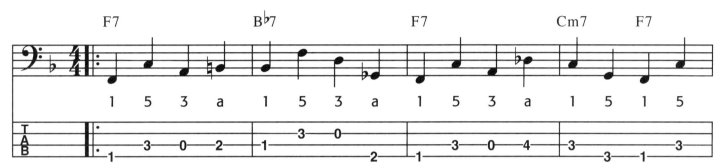

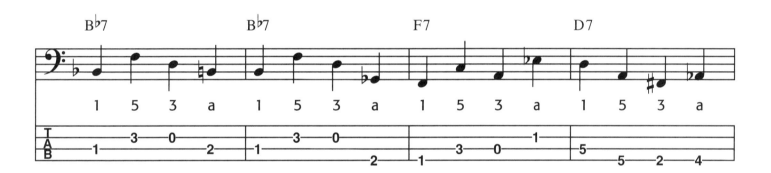

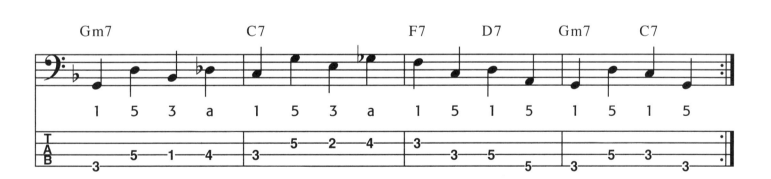

MODULE 25
1–5–3–b

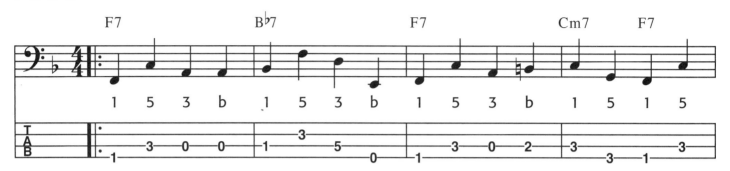

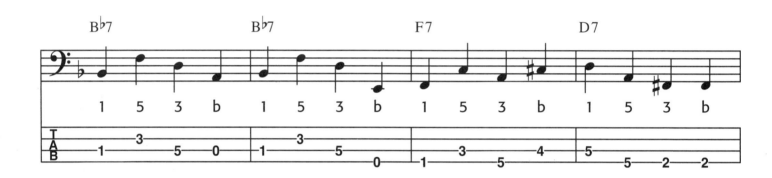

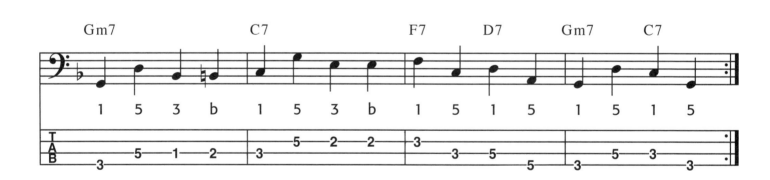

Autumn Leaves

Now that we've finished the first 25 modules and practiced playing each module one module at a time through a chord progression, let's practice plugging two modules into the first eight bars of the popular jazz standard "Autumn Leaves." Here are the chords.

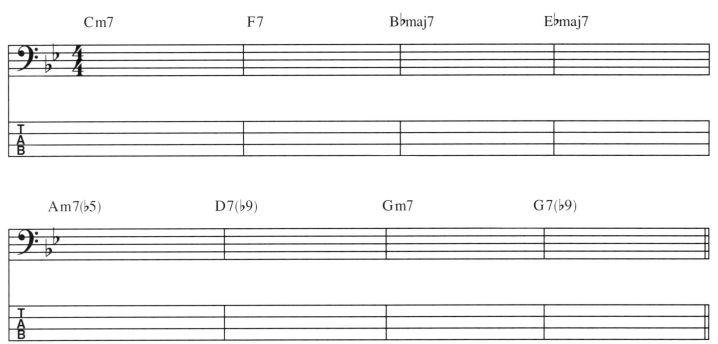

What we're going to do is take module 4 (1–1–5–5) and module 5 (1–1–5–a) and just plug them into every two measures of the chord progression.

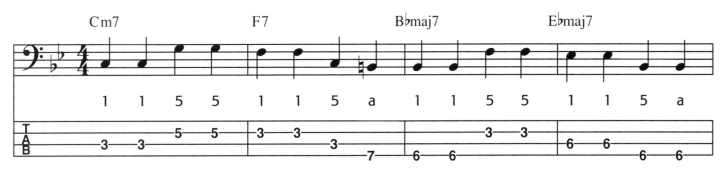

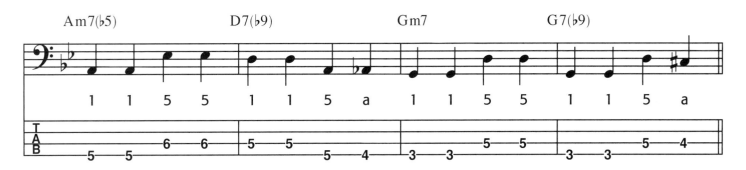

Here's the same chord progression using module 4 (1–1–5–5–) and module 6 (1–1–5–b).

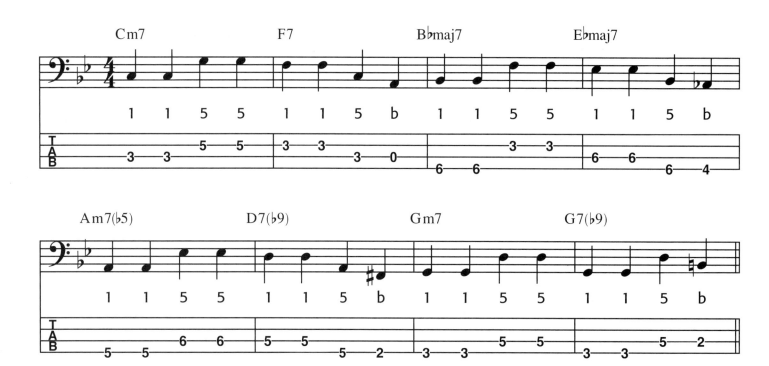

Now, it's up to you to take your favorite modules (or maybe your least favorite as you learn to love them!) and practice this chord progression. Remember: all that it takes is mixing up a handful of these modules and you're well on your way to creating great walking bass lines.

Also, be aware that, later on, we still have to learn scale modules, modal lines, rhythmic articulations, and other devices. Those will all come in subsequent volumes of this series.

MODULE 26

1–3–5–7

Module 26 is not a triad module, as it includes the seventh. Normally, I reserve the seventh for when we study scale modules, but I think it's important that we start moving towards that in this volume.

Let's take a look at this module over the first eight bars of "Autumn Leaves":

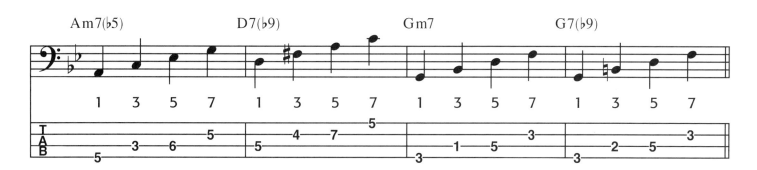

That sounds okay; the notes are correct, but notice that it doesn't resolve smoothly. A smoother way to resolve each measure would be to resolve to the next available chord tone of the next chord. This is a neat little two-bar module for ii–V7 progressions. It is 1–3–5–7 in the first measure to 3–1–7–5 in the second measure; the seventh on beat 4 of the first measure resolves to the third of the chord in the second measure, giving this a very smooth resolution that is almost classical in nature.

MODULE 27

1–3–5–7 | 3–1–7–5

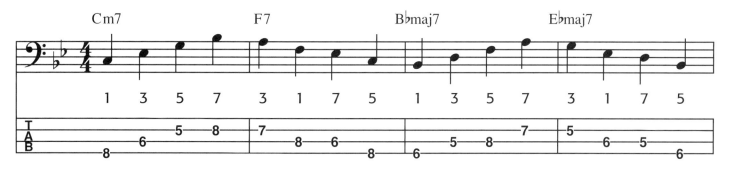

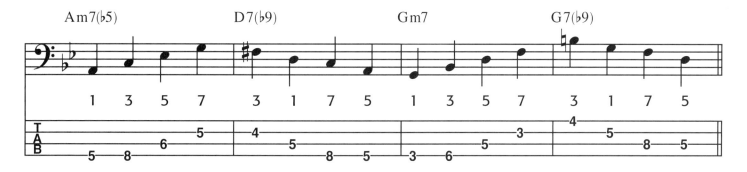

CLOSING THOUGHTS

Remember that this system is designed for you to get in control of some very simple, musical walking bass ideas. Learn them one at a time, over the entire progression, and later on, you should be able to insert them as you see fit. Once you're in control of enough modules, then it's just a matter of inserting a different module every measure, and you're well on your way to completing the picture of the walking bass line.

Modules 1–10 are, in some ways, the hardest, because we have to scope out all the notes on all the beats. Also, remember that these modules have to be **memorized** and **internalized**. I strongly recommend that you play these examples until you can play them 10 times or so without a mistake. If you practice with this kind of diligence, then you should be able to learn modules 1–10 in about one to two weeks. The same should apply to modules 11–20. I recommend another two weeks or so for modules 21–27, with a period of review to follow. So, if you put in the work, you should be "up and walking" in about three to six weeks.

Realize that you can take this module system and plug it into any song that requires a jazz walking bass line. Be sure to experiment taking songs and applying these modules to them. Don't worry about being creative with them at first—just plug them in and play them! You'll find that they work like a charm. After a while, you might find you use some modules more than others, and you might develop a few favorites. Either way, you'll still be on your way to walking in no time!

From now on, it's important that you start checking out other peoples' bass lines. Either check out examples in books, or, better yet, transcribe them yourself. I think you'll discover that these triad modules are all over the place.

Remember that music is a gift from God, so give it the effort, attention, and respect it deserves. Have fun, and play slow!